Children and Their World

A Treasury of Vintage Cuts and Illustrations

Edited by

Judy M. Johnson

DOVER PUBLICATIONS, INC.
New York

Introduction

Though children's magazines of today abound with full-color illustrations, in the early days of children's periodicals production costs (and ultimately costs to the consumer) prohibited much use of color other than on the cover and perhaps a centerfold. This presented a special challenge to illustrators of the day, whose job it was to create images that would enhance the text and inspire the child to turn the next leaf to reveal further treasures. Perhaps because of the "limitations" of black-and-white printing, artists were required to add their touches to every aspect of a publication, from the cover and title page to page headers to stories and poetry to educational articles to toys and games to the final "The End." Their cleverness, variety, and artistry in the use of simple black on white are worthy of our admiration today.

Though much of the material for children in the early decades of this century was educational, flights of fancy and imagination were encouraged, and an abundance of caprice filled these periodicals to make the learning more fun. In this book you will find a broad assortment of banners for the seasons and holidays of the year and for a variety of child-related interests—books, animals, hobbies, games and more. You will find borders as simple as a straight line and as complex as a story illustration. And you will find whimsical vignettes on dozens of fanciful subjects.

Gathering the materials over many years and bringing the illustrations together in this fashion has been a great pleasure. Turning every page of stacks of old volumes in eager anticipation of the next visual enchantment was pure enjoyment. Being an artist myself, I have a particular appreciation for the talents and skills of the artists who created these little wonders. I hope you too will find pleasure, inspiration, and satisfaction in perusing these marvelous illustrations and applying them to your own unique projects.

JUDY M. JOHNSON

Copyright © 1990 by Dover Publications, Inc.
All rights reserved under Pan American and International Copyright Conventions.

Published in Canada by General Publishing Company, Ltd., 30 Lesmill Road, Don Mills, Toronto, Ontario.

Published in the United Kingdom by Constable and Company, Ltd., 3 The Lanchesters, 162–164 Fulham Palace Road, London W6 9ER.

Children and Their World: A Treasury of Vintage Cuts and Illustrations is a new work, first published by Dover Publications, Inc., in 1990.

DOVER *Pictorial Archive* SERIES

Manufactured in the United States of America
Dover Publications, Inc., 31 East 2nd Street, Mineola, N.Y. 11501

Library of Congress Cataloging-in-Publication Data

Children and their world / edited by Judy M. Johnson.
    p.   cm. — (Dover pictorial archive series)
    ISBN 0-486-26457-2
    1. Children's periodicals, American—Illustrations. I. Johnson, Judy M. II. Series.
NC975.C45 1990
745.4′4973′09041—dc20
                                                                    90-36767
                                                                    CIP

NEW YEAR BELLS

January

VALENTINES

February

VALENTINES

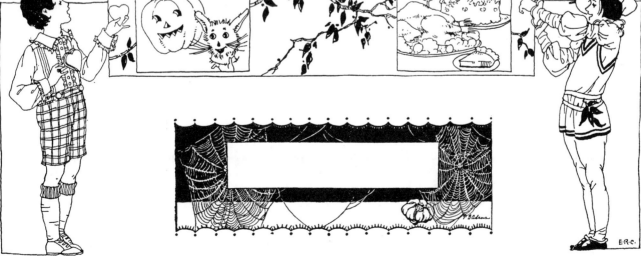

THE
EASTER BUNNY

THE TOYTOWN TATTLER

Price 4 Gumdrops

FUNLAND

HOOHOO CAB

STOP

OUR PETS

May

MOTHER'S DAY

Second Sunday in May

Thanksgiving

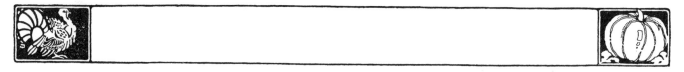

At Christmas Time

Christmas Spirit

CHRISTMAS TREE DECORATIONS

BOOKS BOOKS

OUR BOOK FRIENDS

GEOGRAPHY

Booklovers' Corner

Read-Aloud Time

NELLE FARNAM.

BIBLE STORIES

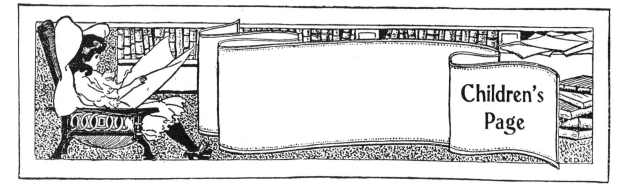

Children's Page

WHO'S WHO in the ZOO

CORINA MELDER-COLLIER

CIRCUS

DOGS

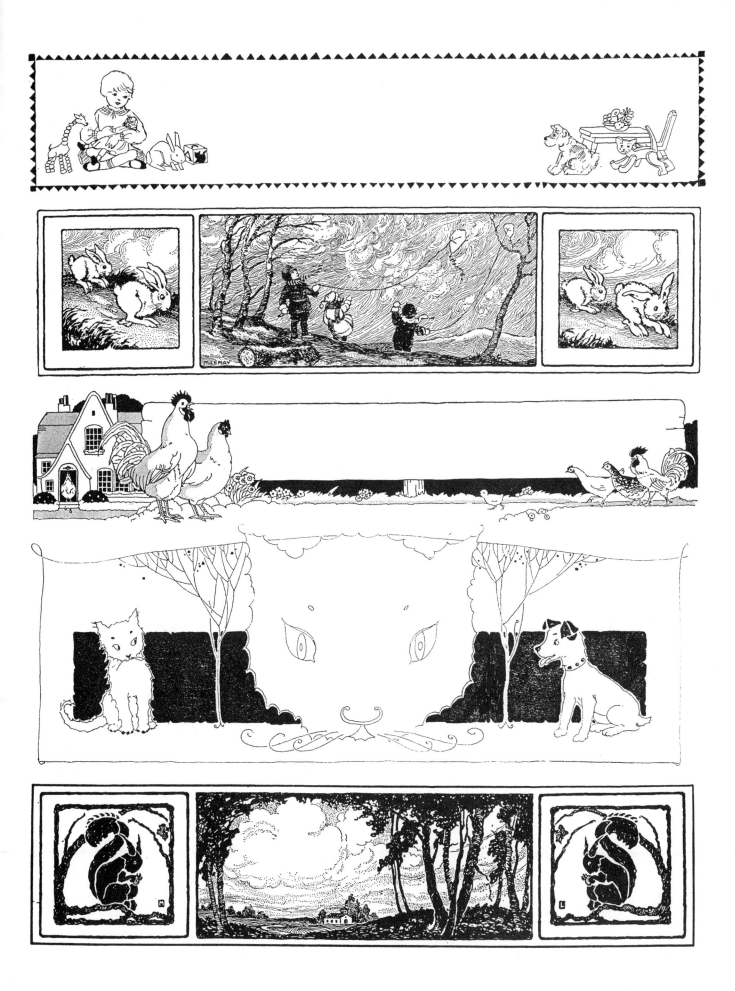

COOKING

GOOD FOODS TO EAT

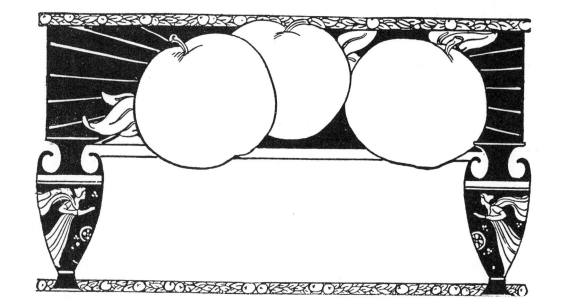

CHILDREN'S KITCHEN

Editor's Page

EDITORIAL

BUSY TIME

Our Workshop

SEWING CIRCLE

GER-
TRUDE A·
STRICKLER

HOBBY CLUB

THE CHILD AND NATURE

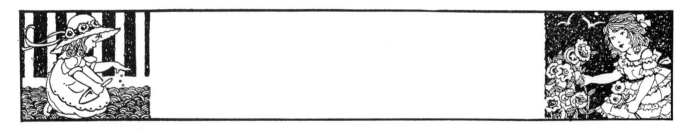

PURPLE MARTINS

WHITE
ELM

TULIP
TREE

WHITE
OAK

PIN
OAK

RED
OAK

BUR
OAK

TO

A FRIEND *of* MINE

OUR POSY PATCH

CAMPS

OUR HEROES

Treasure

Bedtime · Stories

LITTLE BEDTIME STORIES

BEDTIME

OUR BOOK FRIENDS

CLARENCE
BIERS

MILDRED LYUN HETHERINGTON

ETHEL·R·CLINE

EASTER

ETHEL · R · CLINE

KATHERINE
G. HEALEY.

M. Hartwell

The TOYMAKER

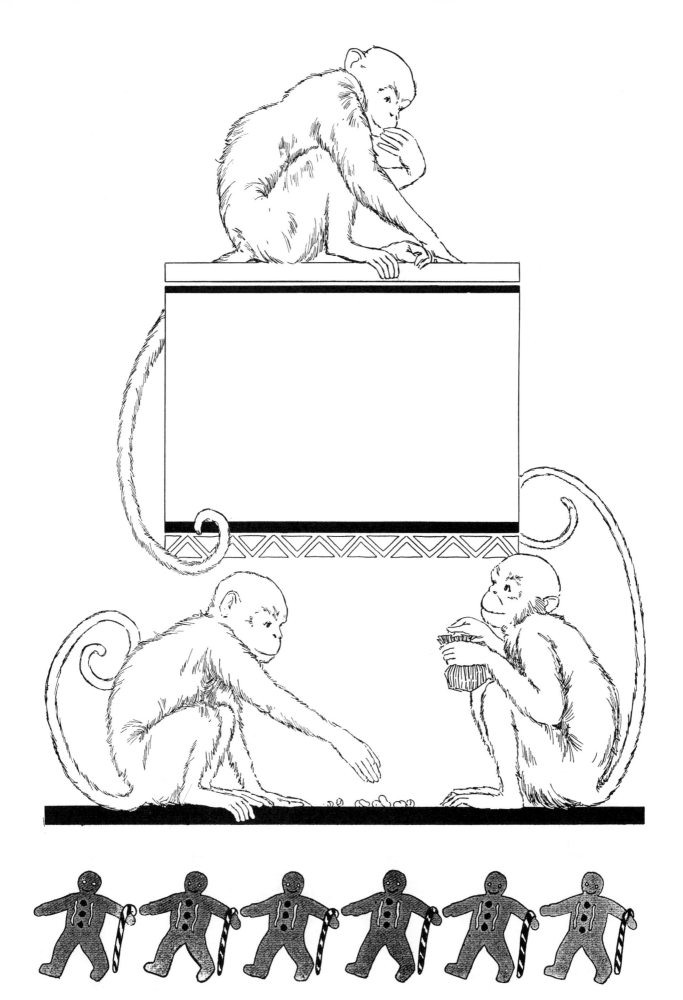

THE END

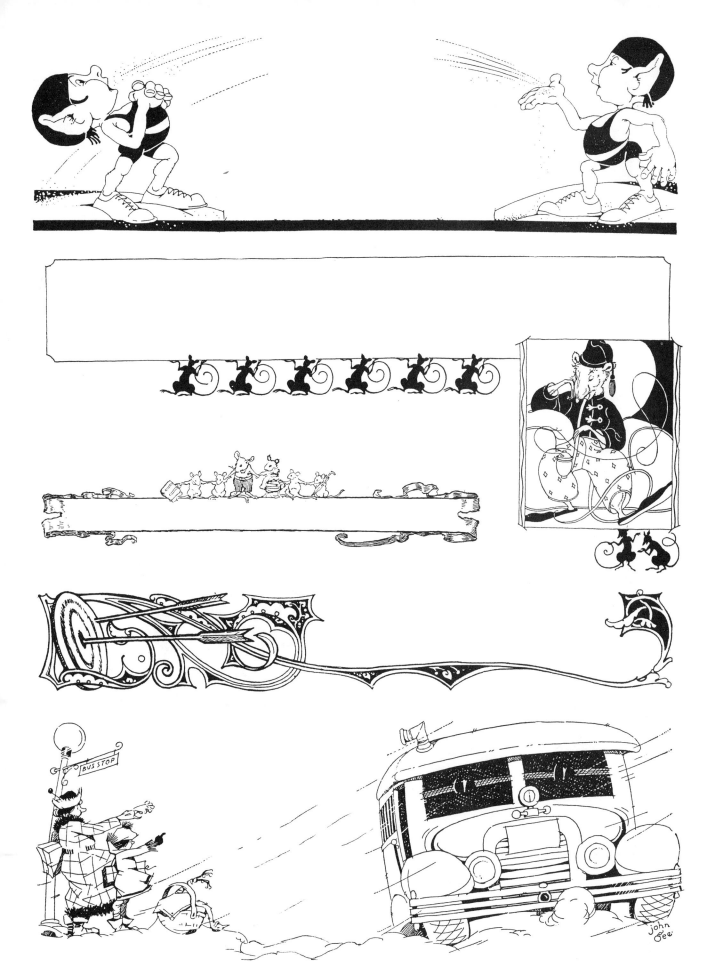

THE NORTH WIND

FLOWERS
and FAIRIES

Lola M. McColl

The Sugar-Plum Tree

Designed by
John Martin

A SONG

Lola M.
McColl

90

CORINA MELDER-COLLIER

EPPIE COLLINS